Wishing you a very

MERRY CHRISTMAS

Happy Holidays

MAY YOUR STAR
SHINE BRIGHT
THIS HOLIDAY
SEASON

WISHING YOU

Peace and Joy

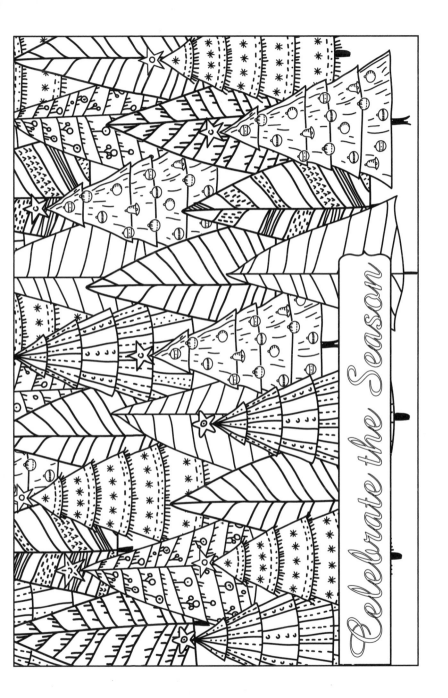

Celebrate the Season

Merry Christmas

Sending you tidings of Comfort and JOY

HAPPY HOLIDAYS

Deck the Halls

MERRY CHRISTMAS

HAPPY NEW YEAR